It's Sunny Today

Kristin Sterling

Lerner Publications Company
Minneapolis

To a little
ray of sunshine—
my niece Kaylee

Lerner Publications Company
A division of Lerner Publishing Group, Inc.
241 First Avenue North
Minneapolis, MN 55401 U.S.A.

Website address: www.lernerbooks.com

Library of Congress Cataloging-in-Publication Data

Sterling, Kristin.
    It's Sunny Today / by Kristin Sterling.
        p.   cm. — (Lightning Bolt Books™—What's the Weather Like?)
    Includes index.
    ISBN 978-0-7613-4259-5 (lib. bdg. : alk. paper)
    1. Solar radiation—Juvenile literature. 2. Summer—Juvenile literature. 3. Sun—Juvenile
literature. I. Title.
    QC911.2.S734 2010
    551.5'271—dc22   2008051583

Manufactured in the United States of America
1 2 3 4 5 6 — BP — 15 14 13 12 11 10

Contents

A Hot, Bright Star

The sun heats Earth. You can swim at the beach.

The sun's rays make lakes and oceans nice and warm for swimming.

Build a mighty sandcastle.
BAM! Knock it down!

The sun lights Earth. You can wear sunglasses.

Sunglasses shade your eyes from bright sunlight.

Put on lots of sunscreen.
Don't forget your ears!

Sunny Seasons

Summer days are long and sunny. The sun goes down around bedtime.

Winter days are short and busy. It gets dark around dinnertime.

Families often eat dinner when it is dark outside in the winter.

Animal Behavior

Animals love sunny days!
Birds sing cheerful songs.

Buzzing bees gather nectar.
Turtles sun themselves on logs.

Turtles like to perch on logs to warm up on sunny days.

Fun in the Sun

Sunny days are happy days! Kids play games in the park.

The weather is perfect for playing outside.

On sunny days, you can see your shadow.

A shadow is an area where light cannot reach because something is blocking its path.

Play shadow tag!

Quick!
Step on your friend's shadow.
Now your friend is it.

On sunny days,
you can eat
sweet ice
cream treats.

You can drink tart lemonade. Mmm—it tastes good!

Lemonade stands are a common sight on sunny summer days.

The Useful Sun

Plants use sunlight to make food. This helps them grow.

Flowers such as daffodils need sunlight to grow.

Wildflowers bloom in open fields. Corn grows tall on farms.

The sun gives Earth energy.
This energy can be used by
people.

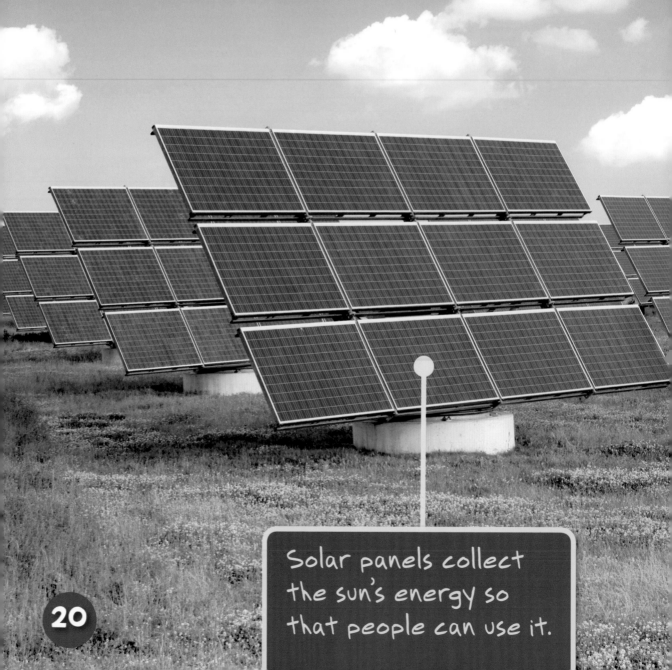

Solar panels collect
the sun's energy so
that people can use it.

Solar energy is used to heat homes and businesses.

Some homes have solar panels on their roofs. The panels turn solar energy into heat.

Is It Hot in Here?

Sunny days can get very hot.

How warm is it?

Measure the temperature with a thermometer.

This student reads a thermometer during a class project.

Some places on Earth have many warm, sunny days. These places are near the equator.

This beach in Brazil is near the equator. The equator is an imaginary line around the middle of Earth.

Other places have few warm, sunny days. These places are near the North Pole and South Pole.

The North Pole (above) and the South Pole are the two farthest points from the equator.

Another Sunny Day

The sun sets in the west.
Another sunny day has ended.

The sun will rise in the east tomorrow. What will you do on the next sunny day?

All about Sun

What Is the Sun?

The sun is an important part of our solar system. It is the star nearest to our planet. It is about 93 million miles (150 kilometers) from Earth. All other stars are much farther away. That is why they look like tiny points of light. The sun is a ball of hot gases. Its center is about 27,000,000°F (15,000,000°C)! It gives off an enormous amount of heat. The sun also produces light. Without light and heat from the sun, there would be no life on our planet.

The Sun and Our Solar System

Mercury

Venus

Earth

Mars

Jupiter

Saturn

Uranus

Neptune

93 million miles between
the sun and Earth

Pluto
(a dwarf
planet)

sun

Glossary

energy: usable power

equator: an imaginary line around the middle of Earth

heat: to make warm

shadow: a dark shape made by something blocking the light

solar: produced by or related to the sun's light and heat

temperature: the degree of heat or cold in something

thermometer: a tool for measuring temperature

Further Reading

Branley, Franklyn M. *The Sun: Our Nearest Star.* New York: HarperCollins, 2002.

Energy Kids' Page: Solar Energy
http://www.eia.doe.gov/kids/energyfacts/sources/renewable/solar.html

Gibbons, Gail. *Weather Words and What They Mean.* New York: Holiday House, 1990.

NASA: Sun for Kids
http://www.nasa.gov/vision/universe/solarsystem/sun_for_kids_main.html

Nelson, Robin. *A Sunny Day.* Minneapolis: Lerner Publications Company, 2002.

Weather Dude
http://www.wxdude.com

Index

Photo Acknowledgments

The images in this book are used with the permission of: © Erik Isakson/Tetra images/Getty Images, p. 1; © Image Source/Getty Images, p. 2; © iStockphoto.com/Rhienna Cutler, p. 4; Reflexstock, p. 5; © iStockphoto.com/Gisele's Gaze, p. 6; © Jochen Sand/Digital Vision/Getty Images, p. 7; © iStockphoto.com/Bradley Mason, p. 8; © Ryan McVay/Photodisc/Getty Images, p. 9; © iStockphoto.com/Paul Tessier, p. 10; © iStockphoto.com/Kevin Beasley , p. 11; © Yellow Dog Productions/Digital Vision/Getty Images/, p. 12; Reflexstock/Blend Images/LWA/Dann Tardif, p. 13; Reflexstock/Radius Images, pp. 14, 15; © iStockphoto.com/Ina Halsor, p. 16; © Photodisc/Getty Images, p. 17; © iStockphoto.com/Jacom Stephens, p. 18; © iStockphoto.com/Justin Voight, p. 19; © iStockphoto.com/Grafissimo, p. 20; © iStockphoto.com/Otmar Smit, p. 21; © Lynne Siler Photography/Alamy, p. 22; © Ellen B. Senisi/The Image Works, p. 23; © Silvestre Machado/SuperStock, p. 24; © Per Breiehagen/The Image Bank/Getty Images, p. 25; © Henrik Sorensen/Stone/Getty Images, p. 26; © iStockphoto.com/Andrew Penner, p. 27; © Laura Westlund/Independent Picture Service, p. 29; © Roine Magnusson/The Image Bank/Getty Images, p. 30; © Peter Dazeley/Digital Vision/Getty Images, p. 31.

Front cover: © Guy Edwardes/Photographer's Choice/Getty Images.